HIP-HOP DANCE

URBAN MOVEMENT

CROWN SHEPHERD
CICELY LEWIS, EXECUTIVE EDITOR

LERNER PUBLICATIONS ◆ MINNEAPOLIS

LETTER FROM CICELY LEWIS

Dear Reader,

Hip-hop has been a part of my life from an early age. I remember using my brush as a microphone and rapping along with Salt-N-Pepa. Hip-hop influenced my fashion, way of speaking, and lifestyle. As a teacher, I shared Tupac's writings to teach poetry elements and Queen Latifah's "U.N.I.T.Y." to help my students better understand the works of poet Maya Angelou.

CICELY LEWIS

As a librarian, I want to expose my students to literature that empowers them to take action and that amplifies voices of underrepresented groups. That is what hip-hop does. Hip-hop is more than beats and rhymes; it's a cultural force. For Black people, it's been a spotlight on social justice, and a canvas for our frustrations, joys, and creativity.

As you read the series, think about the power of hip-hop and how it all began. You've probably heard of Cardi B and Nicki Minaj, but who paved the way for them? Reflect on how this musical genre that began in the Black Community is now present around the world.

—Cicely Lewis, Executive Editor

TABLE OF CONTENTS

BREAKING ON THE WORLD STAGE

B-Boy Phil Wizard breaking at the 2024 Olympics

IN THE SUMMER OF 2024, B-BOYS AND B-GIRLS—BREAK DANCERS OR BREAKERS—TOOK TO THE STAGE TO BATTLE FOR THE GOLD MEDAL AT THE OLYMPICS IN PARIS, FRANCE. It was the first time breakdancing, also known as breaking, appeared in the Olympics. B-Boy Phil Wizard, or Philip Kim, won gold for Canada. B-Girl Ami, or Ami Yuasa, won gold for Japan.

B-Girl Ami competes in the quarterfinals at the 2024 Olympics.

Breakdancing started in the 1970s with Black and Latinx youth of the Bronx in New York City. The sport requires breakers to have physical strength and many athletic skills. Although breaking will not return to the 2028 Olympics, having the sport appear at the Olympics in Paris was a win for breakers and hip-hop culture. It is one way people have celebrated hip-hop's influence on the world.

CHAPTER 1

PARTY HITS

Hip-hop duo Kid 'n Play performing at the Arie Crown Theater in 1989

MANY HIP-HOP DANCES BRING PEOPLE TOGETHER. From school dances to backyard parties, hip-hop dances have been part of countless memories.

FUN STYLE

In 1988 hip-hop duo Kid 'n Play created the dance kick step, also known as the Funky Charleston. Dancers kick one foot forward and step it back while swinging their arms in rhythm with the kicks. The dance was a group creation and one of the most popular dances of the 1990s.

The kick step became popular through Kid 'n Play's music videos for songs such as "Rollin' with Kid 'n Play" and "Do This My Way." The dance and music videos showed their fun and lively style.

Kid 'n Play onstage at Kemper Arena in 1989

EXAGGERATED MOVES

In 1970 Don Campbell created Campbellocking, also known as locking. The dance style involves doing a fast movement and then freezing in place. Then the dancer will do more fast movement. Locking is known for large, exaggerated movements.

Dancers perform a tribute to Don Campbell at the 2021 USA Hip Hop Dance Championship.

69 Boyz take to the stage at the 1995 Source Awards.

GOING PLATINUM

The hip-hop duo 69 Boyz created the dance Tootsee Roll to go with their song of the same name in 1994. As they dance to the beat, dancers lift their heels off the ground and move their knees in and out. They may also switch their weight from one leg to the other.

REFLECT

Some popular hip-hop dances were created by people working together. How can working as a group be helpful in creation?

The dance and song were popular and played at places such as bowling alleys and skating rinks during the 1990s. The song went platinum and reached number 8 on the *Billboard* Hot 100, which charts the week's most popular songs from all genres.

QUICK FEET

During the 1990s, dance crews in Chicago started Footwork, which spread around the world in the 2000s and 2010s. It is a high-energy dance style that focuses on rapid foot movements. Dancers can move their feet more than five beats per second.

Footwork often takes place during dance battles and community events. Dancers form a circle, and one dancer at a time performs in the center of it. DJs and producers in Chicago have played a big role in Footwork by creating songs to match the dance's beat and style.

Dancers practice their moves in 2019.

EMOTIONAL RELEASE

In the early 2000s, Los Angeles dancers Ceasare "Tight Eyez" Willis and Jo'Artis "Big Mijo" Ratti created krumping. Krumping is a high-energy, fast-paced, freestyle dance. It began as a desire to express strong emotions in a positive and nonviolent way.

Ricardo "Boogie Frantick" Rodriguez Jr. krumping in 2012

CHAPTER 2

TOP LINE DANCES

Celeste Jonson and other women dance to the "Cupid Shuffle" at an event in 2019.

A LINE DANCE IS A CHOREOGRAPHED DANCE WHERE A GROUP OF PEOPLE FOLLOW A SERIES OF STEPS. Songs with dance moves in the lyrics have become a hip-hop staple.

TIME TO BOOGIE

In 1976 Bunny Wailer wrote the song "Electric Boogie," and choreographer Ric Silver created a twenty-two-step dance called the Electric Slide. The song and dance became popular when Marcia Griffiths released her remix of the song in 1989. In her music video, Griffiths performed an eighteen-step Electric Slide.

The popular song has been played at weddings, dances, and other events. People of all ages around the world have danced the Electric Slide. In 2023 Griffiths recorded a new version of the "Electric Boogie" for a Jeep commercial. The commercial aired during the Super Bowl and showed animals doing the Electric Slide.

Marcia Griffiths singing in 1990

SLIDE TO THE LEFT

Willie Perry Jr. wrote the "Cha-Cha Slide" in 1998 for a fitness class. The song, also known as "Casper Slide Part 1," was a set of directions on how to do the dance. It's all about having fun and moving with the music.

Willie Perry Jr. on *The Jenny Jones Show* in 2000

Two years later, Perry Jr. released a new version of the song called "Casper Slide Part 2." The new version played on the radio, and the dance became popular for weddings, birthday parties, TV shows, and movies around the world.

REFLECT

Why do you think certain songs remain popular years after they are released? How does dance play a role?

CUPID SHUFFLE

In 2007 Bryson Bernard, or Cupid, wrote "Cupid Shuffle" and created the dance of the same name because he wanted to make a dance for everyone to enjoy. A year later, the Cupid Shuffle set a Guinness World Record for the largest line dance—seventeen thousand people took part in it.

Cupid puts on a performance in 2016.

POPULAR LINE DANCE

In 2008 Victor Grimmy Owusu, also known as V.I.C., created the Wobble line dance to go along with his song "Wobble." To do the Wobble, dancers step side to side with the rhythm of the song, then jump up and move their hips in a circle.

Students and faculty at Howard W. Blake High School do the Wobble in 2014.

"I'm really proud to know the music I'm making has a purpose and that means something to so many people."

—Cupid, 2014

Cupid turned the dance into a workout routine called CuRobiks in 2013. In 2022 the song went five-times platinum. As of 2024, the official "Cupid Shuffle" music video has over 4.7 million views on YouTube.

People doing the Cupid Shuffle

CHAPTER 3

BIG MOMENTS

Hip-hop duo Kriss Kross performing in 1992

SOME HIP-HOP DANCES HAVE REMAINED POPULAR FOR DECADES. They entertain people and inspire other artists to leave a lasting impact.

AN ILLUSION

With millions of people watching, Michael Jackson glided across the stage at the 1983 NBC 25th anniversary celebration for Motown—a record label. Jackson performed what would become his signature dance move: the moonwalk.

The moonwalk was inspired by a popular dance move called the backslide. Jackson learned the moonwalk from some friends and then made it popular in media. The moonwalk is an illusion that makes the dancer appear to be walking forward while they are actually gliding backward.

Michael Jackson in 1983

MAKE PEOPLE JUMP

The 1992 song "Jump" by hip-hop duo Kriss Kross introduced the popular Jump dance to the world. The dance is simple. Dancers jump up and down to the beat.

The song gained international success. It was on *Billboard*'s Hot 100 chart for twenty-one weeks and was at number 1 for eight weeks. The song and dance have been featured in several movies and TV shows. They were also featured in the dancing video game *Just Dance 2*, making people jump decades after the song's release.

LET'S RUN

People debate on who created the running man and who first performed it. Many hip-hop stars have performed the move—where dancers pretend to run in place while pumping their fists in front of them.

In the 1980s, Paula Abdul taught Janet Jackson the running man. Jackson performed the move in her "Rhythm Nation" music video. MC Hammer ran in place in his music video for his 1990 song "U Can't Touch This." He made the running man famous.

Janet Jackson sings and dances in 1989.

In 2016 teens Kevin Vincent and Jeremiah Hall created a social media dance challenge that went viral. People filmed themselves doing the running man.

SURFING ACROSS CROWDS

Hip-hop group Fast Life Yungstaz, or F.L.Y., didn't plan to make a dance when they created the 2009 song "Swag Surfin'." But the song inspired a huge dance craze called swag surfin'. Whenever the song came on, listeners moved side to side together.

Rappers F.L.Y. and Easton perform during the 2023 BET Awards.

Soon after the song's release, videos started popping up on social media of people swag surfin' at parties, concerts, graduations, and sporting events. Fifteen years after the song's release, the dance went viral again when singer Taylor Swift did the dance at a Kansas City Chiefs game. The song was certified platinum in 2024.

REFLECT

What role do you think social media has on hip-hop dances?

CHAPTER 4

DANCE CRAZE

People dance all over the world.

FROM BECOMING POPULAR WORLDWIDE TO GOING VIRAL DECADES AFTER THEIR RELEASE, HIP-HOP DANCES CAN MAKE HISTORY.

WORLD STAR

DJ Webstar and 14-year-old Bianca Bonnie created "Chicken Noodle Soup" in 2006. The song has a dance that includes arm shuffling and moving your feet from side to side. The duo didn't come up with the dance, but Bonnie wrote the song to go with the dance.

Thirteen years after the song's release, j-hope and Becky G remixed "Chicken Noodle Soup." The remix features three languages: Korean, Spanish, and English. As of 2024, the original music video has over seventeen million views, and the music video of the remix has over four hundred million views.

Bianca Bonnie in 2019

"I feel like [the remake] is good for the culture. It was created in Harlem, and now it's a worldwide thing."

—Bianca Bonnie, 2019

Silentó and Heaven perform at the 2016 YouTube Brandcast.

HUGE SUCCESS

"Watch Me (Whip/Nae Nae)" by Silentó became popular in the 2010s. In 2015 Silentó partnered with a group that promotes music and dance on social media. This helped make the dance go viral. To whip, dancers throw their arms out in front of them.

REFLECT

What are some of your favorite hip-hop dances? Why?

Then they nae nae by swinging their hips while waving their hands to the beat.

The song reached number 3 on *Billboard's* Hot 100 and was on the chart for fifty-one weeks. The song's success caught the attention of the record label Capitol Records. They offered Silentó a record deal in 2015.

VIRAL CHALLENGE

"Juju on That Beat (TZ Anthem)" by Zay Hilfigerrr and Zayion McCall went viral in 2016. The dance to the song combines a few different moves. For the main part, dancers pop their shoulders to the song's beat while moving backward and forward on their feet.

Zay Hilfigerrr and Zayion McCall onstage in 2016

Detroit dance duo Fresh The Clowns made the dance popular. They uploaded a version of the dance before the official song or music video was released. The song reached number 5 on the *Billboard* Hot 100.

The popularity of the song and dance also helped land Hilfigerrr and McCall a record deal with Atlantic Records.

THE NEXT CHAPTER

Hip-hop dance has always been about self-expression, community, and trying new things. Artists of the past and present have created dances that have influenced hip-hop and beyond. With new artists and the rise of social media, fans have many more viral dances to look forward to.

Hip-hop fans can look forward to new dances in the future.

MEDLEY

Dancer Fatima Robinson choreographed a medley to end the 2023 Black Entertainment Television Awards on an exciting note. The medley celebrated the fiftieth anniversary of hip-hop by featuring some of the most popular hip-hop dances of all-time. It included Tootsee Roll and swag surfin'.

Fatima Robinson attends an event in 2024.

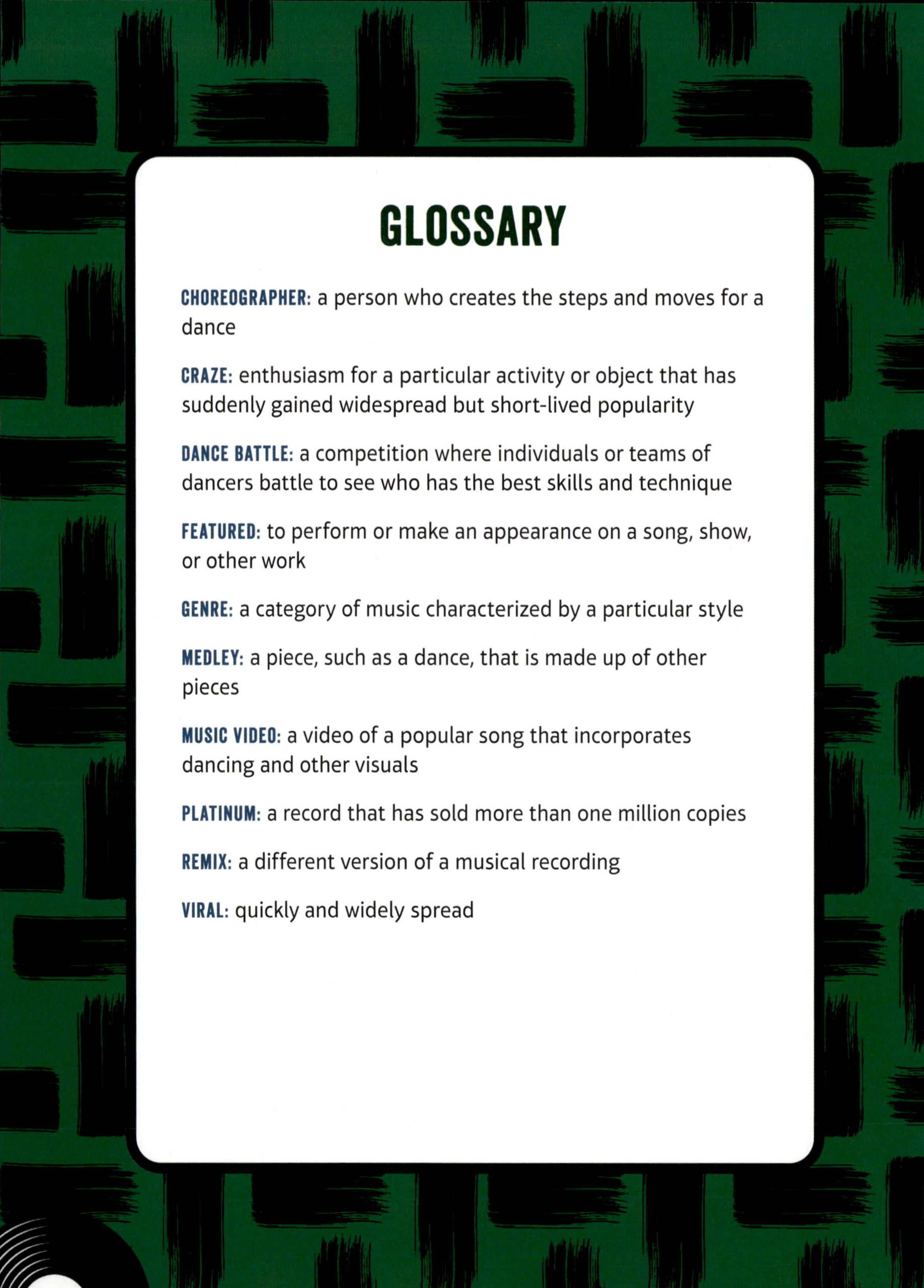

GLOSSARY

CHOREOGRAPHER: a person who creates the steps and moves for a dance

CRAZE: enthusiasm for a particular activity or object that has suddenly gained widespread but short-lived popularity

DANCE BATTLE: a competition where individuals or teams of dancers battle to see who has the best skills and technique

FEATURED: to perform or make an appearance on a song, show, or other work

GENRE: a category of music characterized by a particular style

MEDLEY: a piece, such as a dance, that is made up of other pieces

MUSIC VIDEO: a video of a popular song that incorporates dancing and other visuals

PLATINUM: a record that has sold more than one million copies

REMIX: a different version of a musical recording

VIRAL: quickly and widely spread

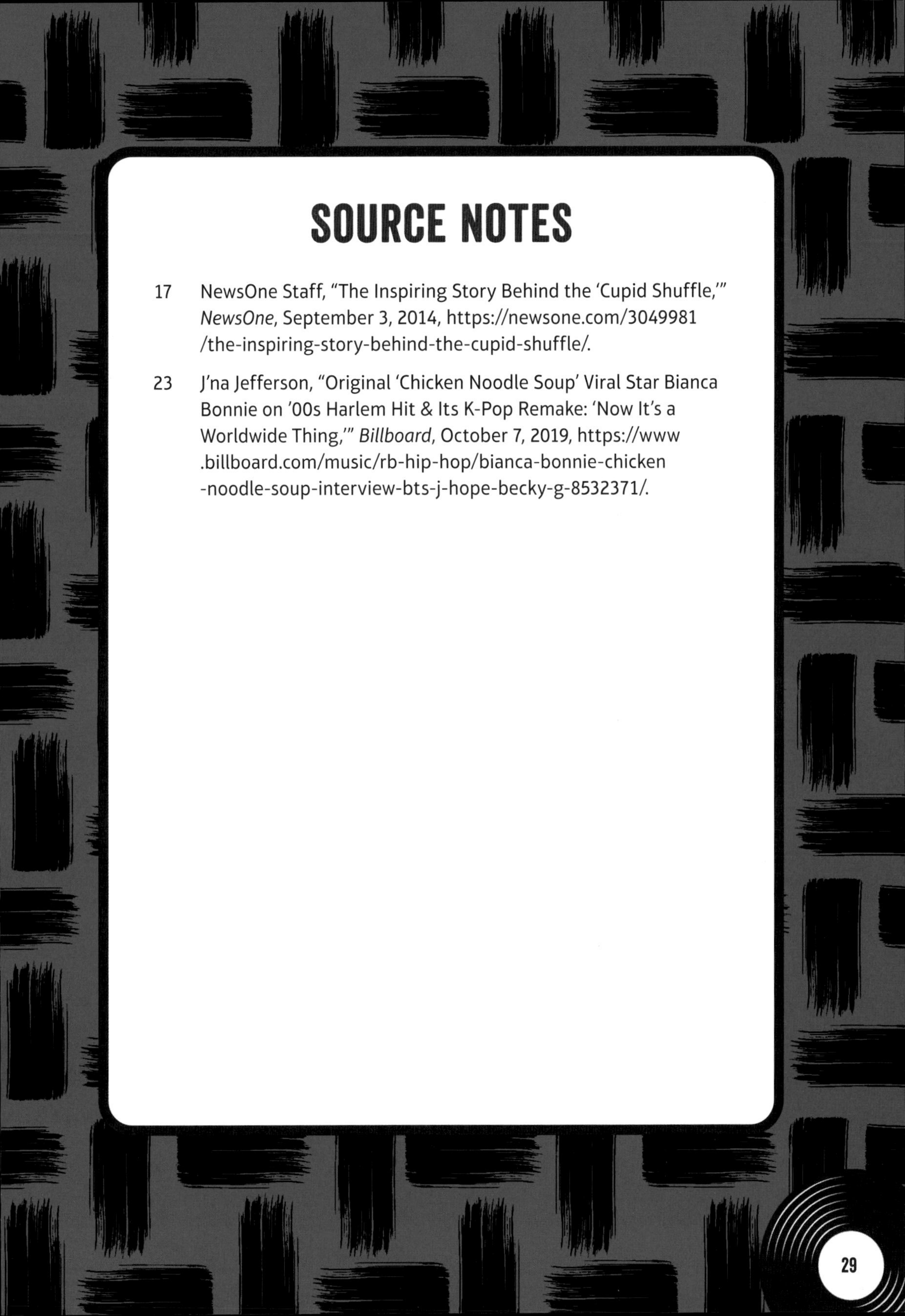

SOURCE NOTES

17 NewsOne Staff, "The Inspiring Story Behind the 'Cupid Shuffle,'" *NewsOne*, September 3, 2014, https://newsone.com/3049981/the-inspiring-story-behind-the-cupid-shuffle/.

23 J'na Jefferson, "Original 'Chicken Noodle Soup' Viral Star Bianca Bonnie on '00s Harlem Hit & Its K-Pop Remake: 'Now It's a Worldwide Thing,'" *Billboard*, October 7, 2019, https://www.billboard.com/music/rb-hip-hop/bianca-bonnie-chicken-noodle-soup-interview-bts-j-hope-becky-g-8532371/.

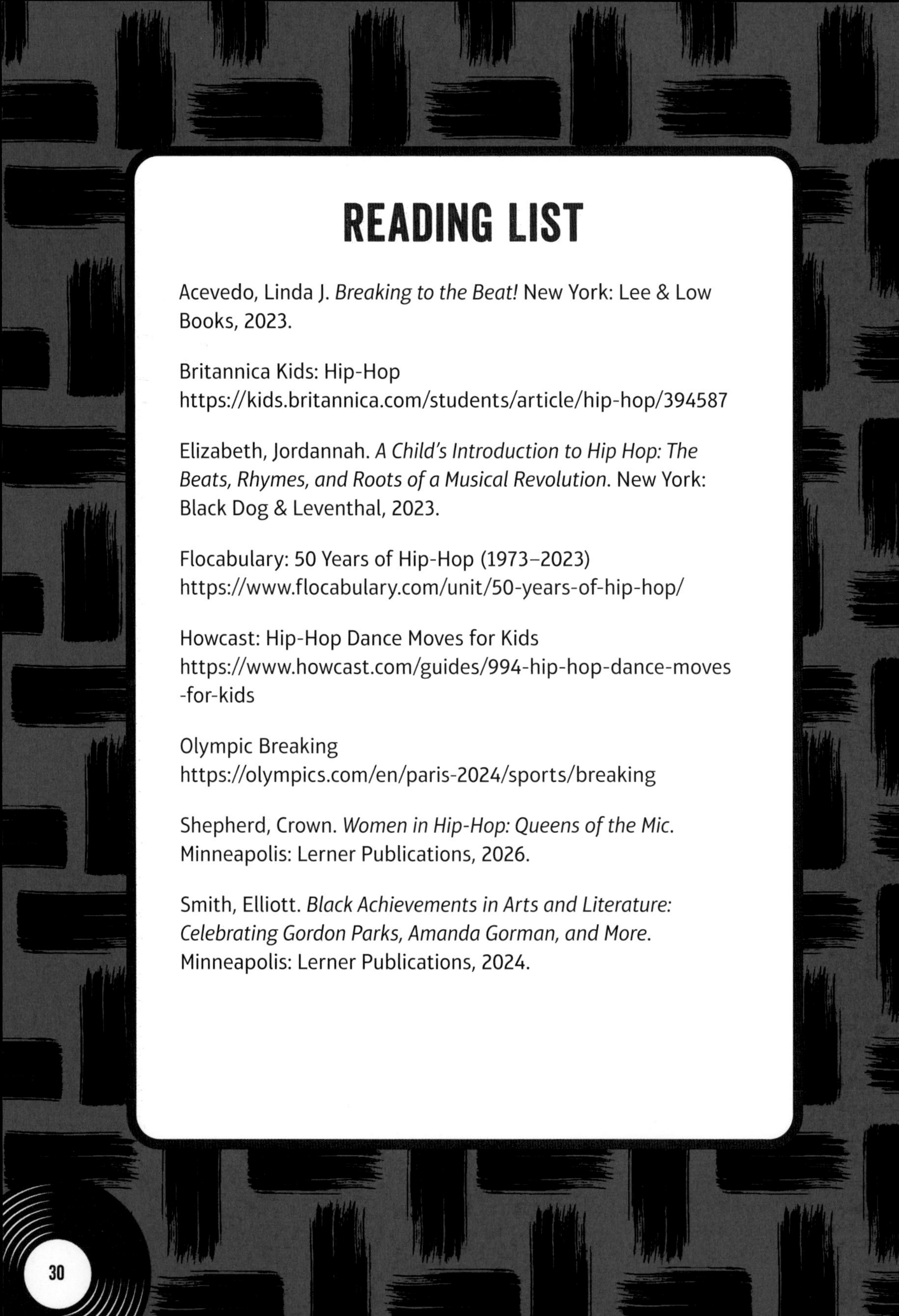

READING LIST

Acevedo, Linda J. *Breaking to the Beat!* New York: Lee & Low Books, 2023.

Britannica Kids: Hip-Hop
https://kids.britannica.com/students/article/hip-hop/394587

Elizabeth, Jordannah. *A Child's Introduction to Hip Hop: The Beats, Rhymes, and Roots of a Musical Revolution*. New York: Black Dog & Leventhal, 2023.

Flocabulary: 50 Years of Hip-Hop (1973–2023)
https://www.flocabulary.com/unit/50-years-of-hip-hop/

Howcast: Hip-Hop Dance Moves for Kids
https://www.howcast.com/guides/994-hip-hop-dance-moves-for-kids

Olympic Breaking
https://olympics.com/en/paris-2024/sports/breaking

Shepherd, Crown. *Women in Hip-Hop: Queens of the Mic*. Minneapolis: Lerner Publications, 2026.

Smith, Elliott. *Black Achievements in Arts and Literature: Celebrating Gordon Parks, Amanda Gorman, and More*. Minneapolis: Lerner Publications, 2024.

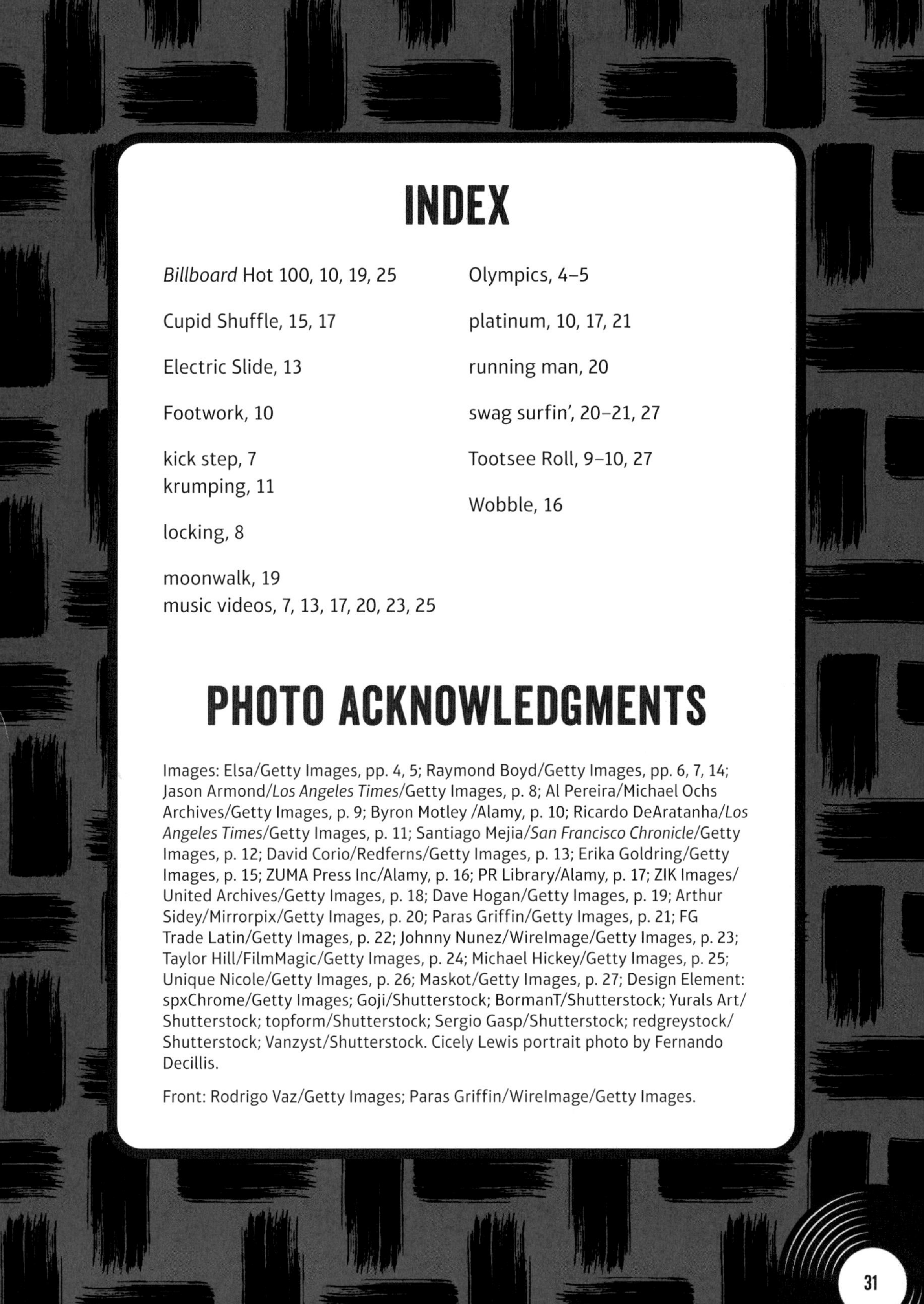

INDEX

PHOTO ACKNOWLEDGMENTS

Images: Elsa/Getty Images, pp. 4, 5; Raymond Boyd/Getty Images, pp. 6, 7, 14; Jason Armond/*Los Angeles Times*/Getty Images, p. 8; Al Pereira/Michael Ochs Archives/Getty Images, p. 9; Byron Motley /Alamy, p. 10; Ricardo DeAratanha/*Los Angeles Times*/Getty Images, p. 11; Santiago Mejia/*San Francisco Chronicle*/Getty Images, p. 12; David Corio/Redferns/Getty Images, p. 13; Erika Goldring/Getty Images, p. 15; ZUMA Press Inc/Alamy, p. 16; PR Library/Alamy, p. 17; ZIK Images/United Archives/Getty Images, p. 18; Dave Hogan/Getty Images, p. 19; Arthur Sidey/Mirrorpix/Getty Images, p. 20; Paras Griffin/Getty Images, p. 21; FG Trade Latin/Getty Images, p. 22; Johnny Nunez/WireImage/Getty Images, p. 23; Taylor Hill/FilmMagic/Getty Images, p. 24; Michael Hickey/Getty Images, p. 25; Unique Nicole/Getty Images, p. 26; Maskot/Getty Images, p. 27; Design Element: spxChrome/Getty Images; Goji/Shutterstock; BormanT/Shutterstock; Yurals Art/Shutterstock; topform/Shutterstock; Sergio Gasp/Shutterstock; redgreystock/Shutterstock; Vanzyst/Shutterstock. Cicely Lewis portrait photo by Fernando Decillis.

Front: Rodrigo Vaz/Getty Images; Paras Griffin/WireImage/Getty Images.

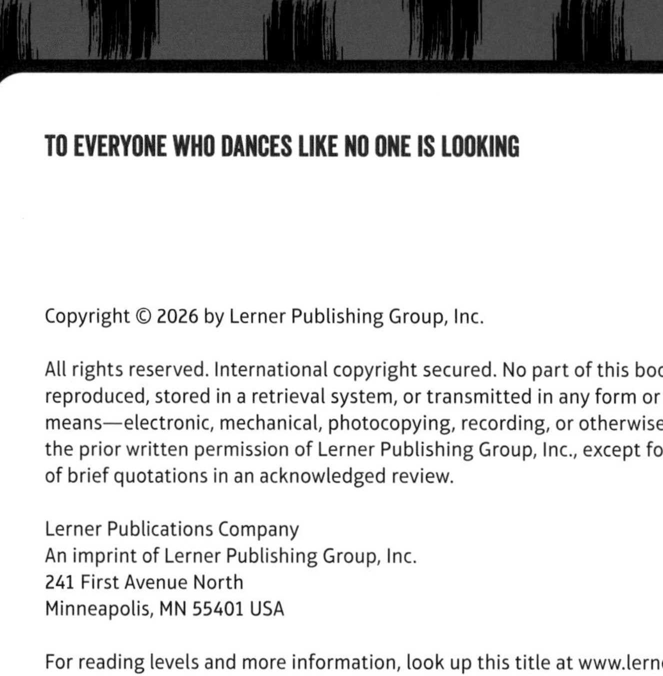

TO EVERYONE WHO DANCES LIKE NO ONE IS LOOKING

Lerner Publications Company
An imprint of Lerner Publishing Group, Inc.
241 First Avenue North
Minneapolis, MN 55401 USA

For reading levels and more information, look up this title at www.lernerbooks.com.

Main body text set in Aptifer Sans LT Pro.
Typeface provided by Linotype AG.

Lerner team: Martha Kranes

Library of Congress Cataloging-in-Publication Data

Names: Shepherd, Crown, author.
Title: Hip-hop dance : urban movement / Crown Shepherd.
Description: Minneapolis, MN : Lerner Publications, [2026] | Series: Hip-hop culture | Includes bibliographical references and index. | Audience: Ages 9–14 | Audience: Grades 4–6 | Summary: "Hip-hop is more than just music. From the first types of hip-hop dances to music videos and dances that have gone viral, readers will explore and celebrate the role dancing has had in hip-hop"— Provided by publisher.
Identifiers: LCCN 2024039719 (print) | LCCN 2024039720 (ebook) | ISBN 9798765659854 (library binding) | ISBN 9798765684252 (paperback) | ISBN 9798765678053 (epub)
Subjects: LCSH: Hip hop dance—Juvenile literature. | Hip-hop—Juvenile literature. | Rap (Music)—Juvenile literature.
Classification: LCC GV1796.H57 S54 2026 (print) | LCC GV1796.H57 (ebook) | DDC 793.3—dc23/eng/20240909

LC record available at https://lccn.loc.gov/2024039719
LC ebook record available at https://lccn.loc.gov/2024039720

Manufactured in the United States of America
1-1011686-53632-2/12/2025